CH

DISCARD

RANDOM HOUSE

TREASURY *of* FRIENDSHIP POEMS

EDITED BY PATRICIA S. KLEIN

RANDOM HOUSE
REFERENCE

New York   Toronto   London   Sydney   Auckland

Visit the Random House Web site: *www.randomhouse.com*
Printed in China
Library of Congress Cataloging-in-Publication Data is available.

First Edition
0 9 8 7 6 5 4 3 2 1

ISBN-10: 0-375-72144-4
ISBN-13: 978-0-375-72144-1

CONTENTS

iv   FOREWORD

1   A Celebration of Friendship

25   Being Friends

47   A Friendly Smile

65   A Place for You by My Side

85   Remembrance of Things Past

107   One Friend to Another

127   Just Good Friends

143   Friends with Fur and Feathers

169   Friendship Lost

191   In Memoriam

211   PERMISSIONS ACKNOWLEDGMENTS

215   INDEX OF AUTHORS

217   INDEX OF FIRST LINES

Friendship

Oh, the comfort—the inexpressible comfort of
  feeling safe with a person,
Having neither to weigh thoughts,
Nor measure words—but pouring them
All right out—just as they are—
Chaff and grain together—
Certain that a faithful hand will
Take and sift them—
Keep what is worth keeping—
And with the breath of kindness
Blow the rest away.

—*Dinah Maria Mulock Craik*

A CELEBRATION OF
FRIENDSHIP ⌒

Of Friendship

Of all the heavenly gifts that mortal men
   commend,
What trusty treasure in the world can
   countervail a friend?
Our health is soon decayed; goods, casual, light
   and vain;
Broke have we seen the force of power, and
   honor suffer stain.
In body's lust man doth resemble but base
   brute;
True virtue gets and keeps a friend, good guide
   of our pursuit,
Whose hearty zeal with ours accords in every
   case;
No term of time, no space of place no storm can
   it deface.
When fickle fortune fails, this knot endureth
   still;

Thy kin out of their kind may swerve, when
   friends owe thee good-will.
What sweeter solace shall befall, than [such a]
   one to find
Upon whose breast thou may'st repose the
   secrets of thy mind?
He waileth at thy woe, his tears with thine be
   shed;
With thee doth he all joys enjoy, so leef a life is
   led.
Behold thy friend, and of thyself the pattern
   see,
One soul, a wonder shall it seem in bodies
   twain to be;
In absence present, rich in want, in sickness
   sound,
Yea, after death alive, mayst thou by thy sure
   friend be found.

Each house, each town, each realm, by thy
　　steadfast love doth stand;
While foul debate breeds bitter bale in each
　　divided land.
O Friendship, flower of flowers! O lively sprite
　　of life!
O sacred bond of blissful peace, the stalworth
　　staunch of strife!

—*Nicholas Grimald*

Who Knows The Joys Of Friendship?

Who knows the joys of friendship?
The trust, the security, and mutual tenderness,
The double joys where each is glad for both?
Friendship, our only wealth, our last retreat
and strength,
Secure against ill fortune and the world.

—*Nicholas Rowe*

Of Perfect Friendship

True friendship unfeignëd
Doth rest unrestrainëd,
　No terror can tame it:
Not gaining, nor losing,
Nor gallant gay glosing,
　Can ever reclaim it.
In pain, and in pleasure,
The most truest treasure
　That may be desirëd,
Is loyal love deemëd,
Of wisdom esteemëd
　And chiefly requirëd.

—*Henry Cheke*

A Friend or Two

There's all of pleasure and all of peace
In a friend or two;
And all your troubles may find release
Within a friend or two;
It's in the grip of the sleeping hand
On native soil or in alien land,
But the world is made—do you understand—
Of a friend or two.

A song to sing, and a crust to share
With a friend or two;
A smile to give and a grief to bear
With a friend or two;
A road to walk and a goal to win,
An inglenook to find comfort in,
The gladdest hours that we know begin
With a friend or two.

A little laughter; perhaps some tears
With a friend or two;
The days, the weeks, and the months and years
With a friend or two;
A vale to cross and a hill to climb,
A mock at age and a jeer at time—
With a friend or two.

The brother-soul and the brother-heart
Of a friend or two
Make us drift on from the crowd apart,
With a friend or two;
For come days happy or come days sad
We count no hours but the ones made glad
By the hale good times we have ever had
With a friend or two.

Then brim the goblet and quaff the toast
To a friend or two,
For glad the man who can always boast
Of a friend or two;
But fairest sight is a friendly face,
The blithest tread is a friendly pace,
And heaven will be a better place
For a friend or two.

—*Wilbur D. Nesbit*

God's Best Gift

What is the best a friend can be
To any soul, to you or me?
Not only shelter, comfort, rest,
Inmost refreshment unexpressed;
Not only a beloved guide
To thread life's labyrinth at our side,
Or with love's torch lead on before—
Though these be much, there yet is more.

The best friend is an atmosphere
Warm with all inspirations dear,
Wherein we breathe the large, free breath
Of life that has no taint of death.
Our friend is an unconscious part
Of every true beat of our heart;
A strength, a growth, whence we derive
God's health, that keeps the world alive.

The best friend is horizon, too,
Lifting unseen things into view,
And widening every pretty claim
Till lost in some sublimer aim;
Blending all barriers in the great
Infinities that round us wait.
Friendship is an eternity
Where soul with soul walks, heavenly free.

Can friend lose friend? Believe it not!
The tissue wherof life is wrought,
Weaving the separate into one,
Nor end hath, nor beginning; spun
From subtle threads of destiny,
Finer than thought of man can see.
God takes not back his gifts divine;
While thy soul lives, thy friend is thine.

If but one friend crossed thy way,
Once only, in thy mortal day;
If only once life's best surprise
Has opened on thy human eyes—
Ingrate thou wert, indeed if thou
Didst not in that rare presence bow,
And on Earth's holy ground unshod,
Speak softlier the dear name of *God*.

—*Lucy Larcom*

Friendship

Friendship. peculiar boon of heav'n,
The noble mind's delight and pride,
To men and angels only giv'n,
To all the lower world denied.

Thy gentle flows of guiltless joys
On fools and villians ne'er descend;
In vain for thee the tyrant sighs,
And hugs a flatterer for a friend.

Directress of the brave and just,
O guide us through life's darksome way!
And let the tortures of mistrust
On selfish bosoms only prey.

Nor shall thine ardors cease to glow,
When souls to peaceful climes remove:
What rais'd our virtue here below,
Shall aid our happiness above.

—*Samuel Johnson*

To Friendship

Oh! Friendship, sweetest, exquisite delight,
　　For fine according spirits formed alone!
'Tis thine our feeling bosoms to unite,
　　And youthful hearts thy melting ardours own.

To give the mind its animated glow,
　　Kindle the languid virtues to a flame,
To bid the genial tear of pity flow,
　　To raise the "blushes of ingenuous shame,"

These arts, oh! child of sympathy, are thine;
　　And I will bless thy consecrated power;
Will pour my early offering at thy shrine,
　　And oft invoke thee in the pensive hour.

Ah! when our brightest prospects fade away,
　　And Hope shall cease her glowing hues to
　　　　blend:
Then, when the bright illusive scenes decay,
　　'Tis then we prove the blessings of a friend.

Diffuse thy influence o'er my youthful mind,
  The artless song I dedicate to thee;
What pleasing sorrows oft in thee we find,
  Oh! child of tender sensibility.

With thee in pensive pleasure I would melt;
  To me thy raptures, thy endearments give:
Oh! ye, who these according joys have felt,
  Say, with a generous friend, how sweet to
    grieve.

Oh! yes, we love our sorrows to impart,
And meet our comfort from a kindred heart;
The elevated soul, by thee refined,
Once to thy dear enchanting sway resigned,
Shall ever pour the genuine vow to thee,
Oh! child of tender sensibility.

—*Felicia Dorothea Hemans*

It Is a Sweet Thing

It is a sweet thing, friendship, a dear balm,
A happy and auspicious bird of calm,
Which rides o'er life's ever tumultuous Ocean;
A God that broods o'er chaos in commotion;
A flower which fresh as Lapland roses are,
Lifts its bold head into the world's frore air,
And blooms most radiantly when others die,
Health, hope, and youth, and brief prosperity;
And with the light and odour of its bloom,
Shining within the dungeon and the tomb;
Whose coming is as light and music are
'Mid dissonance and gloom—a star
Which moves not 'mid the moving heavens
   alone—
A smile among dark frowns—a gentle tone
Among rude voices, a beloved light,
A solitude, a refuge, a delight.

—*Percy Bysshe Shelley*

I Love Life in All Its Phases

I love life in all its phases,
   I love it for the joy it brings—
The starry nights—the trees that grow,
   The song of a bird as it sings.

I love life—its compensations
   Give courage and strength to be glad
When sorrow and disappointment
   Would render me lonely and sad.

I love life—because of friendships—
   The understanding hearts that feel
My need of closer fellowship
   When darkest hours o'er me steal.

I love life—and I want to live,
   Until all of my dreams come true—
Till I can prove to all the world,
   The darkest cloud is lined with blue.

—*Ruth A. Hartzell*

Friends

Now must I these three praise—
Three women that have wrought
What joy is in my days:
One because no thought,
Nor those unpassing cares,
No, not in these fifteen
Many-times-troubled years,
Could ever come between
Mind and delighted mind;
And one because her hand
Had strength that could unbind
What none can understand,
What none can have and thrive,
Youth's dreamy load, till she
So changed me that I live
Labouring in ecstasy.
And what of her that took
All till my youth was gone

With scarce a pitying look?
How could I praise that one?
When day begins to break
I count my good and bad,
Being wakeful for her sake,
Remembering what she had,
What eagle look still shows,
While up from my heart's root
So great a sweetness flows
I shake from head to foot.

—*William Butler Yeats*

The Human Touch

'Tis the human touch in this world that counts,
  The touch of your hand and mine,
Which means far more to the fainting heart
  Than shelter and bread and wine.
For shelter is gone when the night is o'er,
  And bread lasts only a day,
But the touch of the hand and the sound of the
    voice
  Sing on in the soul alway.

—*Spencer Michael Free*

A Song

(Written in her fifteenth year.)

Life is but a troubled ocean,
Hope a meteor, love a flower
Which blossoms in the morning beam,
And withers with the evening hour.

Ambition is a dizzy height,
And glory, but a lightning gleam;
Fame is a bubble, dazzling bright,
Which fairest shines in fortune's beam.

When clouds and darkness veil the skies,
And sorrow's blast blows loud and chill,
Friendship shall like a rainbow rise,
And softly whisper—peace, be still.

—*Lucretia Maria Davidson*

They Say That in the Unchanging Place

(from Dedicatory Ode)

They say that in the unchanging place,
   Where all we loved is always dear,
We meet our morning face to face
   And find at last our twentieth year . . .

They say (and I am glad they say)
   It is so; and it may be so:
It may be just the other way,
   I cannot tell. But this I know:

From quiet homes and first beginning,
   Out to the undiscovered ends,
There's nothing worth the wear of winning,
   But laughter and the love of friends

—*Hilaire Belloc*

The Pleasures of Friendship

The pleasures of friendship are exquisite,
How pleasant to go to a friend on a visit!
I go to my friend, we walk on the grass,
And the hours and moments like minutes pass.

—*Stevie Smith*

BEING FRIENDS

On Friendship

And a youth said, Speak to us of Friendship.
And he answered, saying:
Your friend is your needs answered.
He is your field which you sow with love and
    reap with thanksgiving.
And he is your board and your fireside.
For you come to him with your hunger, and you
    seek him for peace.

When your friend speaks his mind you fear not
    the "nay" in your own mind, nor do you
    withhold the "ay."
And when he is silent your heart ceases not to
    listen to his heart;
For without words, in friendship, all thoughts,
    all desires, all expectations are born and
    shared, with joy that is unacclaimed.
When you part from your friend, you grieve not;
For that which you love most in him may be
    clearer in his absence, as the mountain to the
    climber is clearer from the plain.

And let there be no purpose in friendship save
the deepening of the spirit.
For love that seeks aught but the disclosure of
its own mystery is not love but a net cast
forth: and only the unprofitable is caught.

And let your best be for your friend.
If he must know the ebb of your tide, let him
know its flood also.
For what is your friend that you should seek
him with hours to kill?
Seek him always with hours to live.
For it is his to fill your need, but not your
emptiness.
And in the sweetness of friendship let there be
laughter, and sharing of pleasures.
For in the dew of little things the heart finds its
morning and is refreshed.

—*Kahlil Gibran*

True Friends

True friends,
Like ivy and the wall
Both stand together,
And together fall.

—*Thomas Carlyle*

New Friends and Old Friends

Make new friends, but keep the old;
Those are silver, these are gold.
New-made friendships, like new wine,
Age will mellow and refine.
Friendships that have stood the test—
Time and change—are surely best;
Brow may wrinkle, hair grow gray,
Friendship never knows decay.
For 'mid old friends tried and true,
Once more we our youth renew.
But old friends, alas may die,
New friends must their place supply.
Cherish friendship in your breast—
New is good, but old is best;
Make new friends, but keep the old;
Those are silver, these are gold.

—*Joseph Parry*

Friendship; A Sonnet

As when with downcast eyes we muse and
   brood,
And ebb into a former life, or seem
To lapse far back in some confused dream
To states of mystical similitude,
If one but speaks or hems or stirs his chair,
Ever the wonder waxeth more and more,
So that we say, "All this hath been before,
All this hath been, I know not when or where";
So, friend, when first I look'd upon your face,
Our thought gave answer each to each, so true—
Opposed mirrors each reflecting each—
That, tho I knew not in what time or place,
Methought that I had often met with you,
And either lived in either's heart and speech.

—*Alfred, Lord Tennyson*

The Thousandth Man

One man in a thousand, Solomon says,
   Will stick more close than a brother.
And it's worth while seeking him half your days
   If you find him before the other.
Nine hundred and ninety-nine depend
   On what the world sees in you,
But the Thousandth Man will stand your friend
   With the whole round world agin you.

'Tis neither promise nor prayer nor show
   Will settle the finding for 'ee.
Nine hundred and ninety-nine of 'em go
   By your looks or your acts or your glory.
But if he finds you and you find him,
   The rest of the world don't matter;
For the Thousandth Man will sink or swim
   With you in any water.

You can use his purse with no more shame
    Than he uses yours for his spendings;
And laugh and mention it just the same
    As though there had been no lendings.
Nine hundred and ninety-nine of 'em call
    For silver and gold in their dealings;
But the Thousandth Man he's worth 'em all,
    Because you can show him your feelings!

His wrong's your wrong, and his right's your
        right,
    In season or out of season.
Stand up and back it in all men's sight—
    With that for your only reason!
Nine hundred and ninety-nine can't bide
    The shame or mocking or laughter,
But the Thousandth Man will stand by your side
    To the gallows-foot—and after!

—*Rudyard Kipling*

Friendship

To meet a friendship such as mine,
Such feelings must thy soul refine,
As are not oft of mortal birth;—
'Tis love without a stain of earth,
    Fratello del mio cor.
Looks are its food, its nectar sighs,
Its couch the lips, its throne the eyes,
The soul its breath, and so possest,
Heaven's raptures reign in mortal breast,
    Fratello del mio cor.
Though friendship be its earthly name,
Purely from highest heaven it came;
'Tis seldom felt for more than one,
And scorns to dwell with Venus' son,
    Fratello del mio cor.
Him let it view not, or it dies
Like tender hues of morning skies,
Or morn's sweet flower of purple glow,

When sunny beams too ardent grow,
   Fratello del mio cor.
A charm o'er every object plays—
All looks so lovely, while it stays,
So softly forth in rosier tides,
The vital flood ecstatic glides,
   Fratello del mio cor,
That wrung by grief to see it part,
A very life drop leaves the heart;
Such drop, I need not tell thee, fell.
While bidding it for thee, farewell.
   Fratello del mio cor.

—*Maria A. Brooks*

Faults

They came to tell your faults to me,
They named them over one by one;
I laughed aloud when they were done,
I knew them all so well before,—
Oh, they were blind, too blind to see
Your faults had made me love you more.

—*Sara Teasdale*

Friendship

Friendship needs no studied phrases,
Polished face, or winning wiles;
Friendship deals no lavish praises,
Friendship dons no surface smiles.

Friendship follows Nature's diction,
Shuns the blandishments of Art,
Boldly severs truth from fiction,
Speaks the language of the heart.

Friendship favors no condition,
Scorns a narrow-minded creed,
Lovingly fulfills its mission,
Be it word or be it deed.

Friendship cheers the faint and weary,
Makes the timid spirit brave,
Warns the erring, lights the dreary,
Smoothes the passage to the grave.

Friendship—pure, unselfish friendship,
All through life's allotted span,
Nurtures, strengthens, widens, lengthens
Man's relationship with man.

—*Anonymous*

Friendship

I think awhile of Love, and while I think,
  Love is to me a world,
  Sole meat and sweetest drink,
  And close connecting link
    Tween heaven and earth.

I only know it is, not how or why,
  My greatest happiness;
  However hard I try,
  Not if I were to die,
    Can I explain.

I fain would ask my friend how it can be,
  But when the time arrives,
  Then Love is more lovely
  Than anything to me,
    And so I'm dumb.

For if the truth were known, Love cannot speak,
    But only thinks and does;
    Though surely out 'twill leak
    Without the help of Greek,
      Or any tongue.

A man may love the truth and practise it,
    Beauty he may admire,
    And goodness not omit,
    As much as may befit
      To reverence.

But only when these three together meet,
    As they always incline,
    And make one soul the seat,
    And favorite retreat
      Of loveliness;

When under kindred shape, like loves and hates
    And a kindred nature,
    Proclaim us to be mates,
    Exposed to equal fates
        Eternally;

And each may other help, and service do,
    Drawing Love's bands more tight,
    Service he ne'er shall rue
    While one and one make two,
        And two are one;

In such case only doth man fully prove
    Fully as man can do,
    What power there is in Love
    His inmost soul to move
        Resistlessly.

Two sturdy oaks I mean, which side by side,
   Withstand the winter's storm,
   And spite of wind and tide,
   Grow up the meadow's pride,
      For both are strong

Above they barely touch, but undermined
   Down to their deepest source,
   Admiring you shall find
   Their roots are intertwined
      Insep'rably.

—*Henry David Thoreau*

I Saw in Louisiana
a Live Oak Growing

I saw in Louisiana a live-oak growing,
All alone stood it and the moss hung down
    from the branches,
Without any companion it grew there uttering
    joyous leaves of dark green,
And its look, rude, unbending, lusty, made me
    think of myself,
But I wonder'd how it could utter joyous leaves
    standing alone there without its friends, for I
    knew I could not,
And I broke off a twig with a certain number of
    leaves upon it, and twined around it a little
    moss,
And brought it away, and I have placed it in
    sight in my room.
It is not needed to remind me as of my own
    dear friends,

(For I believe lately I think of little else than of
   them)
Yet it remains to me a curious token, it makes
   me think of manly love;
For all that, and though the live-oak glistens
   there in Louisiana solitary in a wide flat space,
Uttering joyous leaves all its life without a
   friend or a lover near,
I know very well I could not.

—*Walt Whitman*

Friendship's Like Music

Friendship's like music; two strings tuned alike,
Will both stir, though but only one you strike.
It is the quintessence of all perfection
Extracted into one: a sweet connection
Of all the virtues moral and divine,
Abstracted into one. It is a mine,
Whose nature is not rich, unless in making
The state of others wealthy, by partaking.
It blooms and blossoms both in sun and shade,
Doth (like a bay in winter) never fade:
It loveth all, and yet suspecteth none,
Is provident, yet seeketh not her own;
'Tis rare itself, yet maketh all things common;
And is judicious, yet judgeth no man.

*   *   *

The perfect model of true friendship's this:
A rare affection of the soul, which is
Begun with ripened judgment; doth perséver
With simple wisdom, and concludes with
  Never.
'Tis pure in substance, as refined gold,
That buyeth all things, but is never sold,
It is a coin, and most men walk without it;
True love's the stamp, Jehovah's writ about it;
It rusts unused, but using makes it brighter,
'Gainst Heaven high treason 'tis to make it
  lighter.

—*Francis Quarles*

Music and Friendship

Thrice is sweet music sweet when every word
And lovely tone by kindred hearts are heard;
So when I hear true music, Heaven send,
To share that heavenly joy, one dear, dear friend!

—*Richard Watson Gilder*

A FRIENDLY SMILE ⌒

An Epigram

You meet your friend, your face
Brightens—you have struck gold.

—Kassia

Fellowship

When a feller hasn't got a cent
And is feelin' kind of blue,
And the clouds hang thick and dark
And won't let the sunshine through,
It's a great thing, oh my brethren,
For a feller just to lay
His hand upon your shoulder in a
   friendly sort o' way.

It makes a man feel happy,
It makes the tear-drops start.
And you kind o' feel a flutter
In the region of your heart.
You can't look up and meet his eye,
You don't know what to say
When a hand is on your shoulder in a
   friendly sort o' way.

Oh, this world's a curious compound
With its honey and its gall;
Its cares and bitter crosses,
But a good world after all.
And a good God must have made it,
Leastwise that is what I say,
When a hand is on your shoulder in a
    friendly sort o' way.

—*Author unknown*

Silence

'Tis better to sit here beside the sea,
Here, on the spray-kissed beach,
In silence, that between such friends as we
Is full of deepest speech.

—*Paul Laurence Dunbar*

Friendship

If you're ever in a jam, here I am.
If you're ever in a mess, S.O.S.
If you're so happy, you land in jail. I'm your bail.
   It's friendship, friendship, just a perfect
      blendship.
   When other friendships are soon forgot, ours
      will still be hot.

If you're ever up a tree, phone to me.
If you're ever down a well, ring my bell.
If you ever lost your teeth and you're out to
      dine, borrow mine.
   It's friendship, friendship, just a perfect
      blendship.
   When other friendships are soon forgate, ours
      will still be great.

If they ever black your eyes, put me wise.
If they ever cook your goose, turn me loose.
And if they ever put a bullet through your
   brain, I'll complain.
  It's friendship, friendship, just a perfect
   blendship.
  When other friendships are soon forgit, ours
   will still be it.

If you ever lose your mind, I'll be kind.
And if you ever lose your shirt, I'll be hurt.
If you're ever in a mill and get sawed in half,
   I won't laugh.
  It's friendship, friendship, just a perfect
   blendship.
  When other friendships are are up the crick,
   ours will still be slick.

—*Cole Porter*

A Little Health

A little health,
A little wealth,
A little house and freedom,
And at the end
A little friend
And little cause to need him.

—*Anonymous*
Recorded in The Diary of Francis Kilvert *(1870–1879)*

A Time to Talk

When a friend calls to me from the road
And slows his horse to a meaning walk,
I don't stand still and look around
On all the hills I haven't hoed,
And shout from where I am, What is it?
No, not as there is a time to talk.
I thrust my hoe in the mellow ground,
Blade-end up and five feet tall,
And plod: I go up to the stone wall
For a friendly visit.

—*Robert Frost*

Take Care of Yer Friends

Friend is a word that I don't throw around
Though it's used and abused, I still like the
sound.
I save it for people who've done right by me
And I know I can count on if ever need be.

Some of my friends drive big limousines
Own ranches and banks and visit with queens.
And some of my friend are up to their neck
In overdue notes and can't write a check.

They're singers or ropers or writers of prose
And others, God bless'em, can't blow their own
nose!
I guess bein' friends don't have nothin' to do
With talent or money or knowin' who's who.

It's a comf'terbul feelin' when you don't have to
care
'Bout choosin' your words or bein' quite fair
'Cause friends'll just listen and let go on by
Those words you don't mean and not bat an eye.

It makes a friend happy to see your success.
They're proud of yer good side and forgive all
  the rest
And that ain't so easy, all of the time
Sometimes I get crazy and seem to go blind!

Yer friends just might have to take you on home
Or remind you sometime that you're not alone.
Or ever so gently pull you back to the ground
When you think you can fly with no one
  around.

A hug or a shake, whichever seems right
Is the high point of givin', I'll tellya tonight,
All worldly riches and tributes of men
Can't hold a candle to the worth of a friend.

—*Baxter Black*

My Buddy

Life is a book that we study,
Some of its leaves bring a sigh,
There it was written, my buddy,
That we must part, you and I.

Chorus:
Nights are long since you went away,
I think about you all through the day,
My buddy, my buddy, no buddy quite so true.
Miss your voice, the touch of your hand,
Just long to know that you understand,
My buddy, my buddy, your buddy misses you

Buddies through all the gay days,
Buddies when something went wrong;
I wait alone through the gray days,
Missing your smile and your song.

Chorus:
Nights are long since you went away,
I think about you all through the day,
My buddy, my buddy, no buddy quite so true.
Miss your voice, the touch of your hand,
Just long to know that you understand,
My buddy, my buddy, your buddy misses you

—Gus Kahn

"As You're a Friend—"

"You're a friend of mine, or I wouldn't ask,"
And he straightway assigned a thankless task
That he shied from himself, a disreputable job
The offer of which would insult a lob
He would have to pay. "As a friend," he said:
I did it of course, but I still see red.
Of all sins I swear that this most will I shun—
Using friendship's name to get dirty work
    done.

—*St. Clair Adams*

Oh Lucky Jim

Jim and I as children played together,
  Best of friends for many years were we
I, alas! had no luck, was a Jonah,
  Jim, my chum, was lucky as could be.
    Oh lucky Jim, how I envy him!

Years passed by, still Jim and I were comrades.
  He and I both loved the same sweet maid.
She loved Jim, and married him one evening.
  Jim was lucky, I unlucky stayed.
    Oh lucky Jim, how I envy him!

Years rolled on, and death took Jim away, boys,
  Left his widow, and she married me.
Now we're married, oft I think of Jim, boys,
  Sleeping in the churchyard, peacefully.
    Oh lucky Jim, how I envy him!

—*Anonymous*

Throwing Out Old Clothes

Throwing out old clothes is painful, because
how do I know I won't need them again?
This one, discolored under the arms, was
worn to dinner—roast duck—with two old
   friends.
It smells creaky, like floorboards smell; the closet
where it's been jammed smells of bits of stain
   (duck
à l'orange, crab, pork, veal) dried, pressed, and set
into a now-napless cloth. Time to chuck
the lot. What I need again are the friends,
not the clothes, though *they* were friends. One
   woman
moved back to her hometown and remarried.
That one I sewed, then let fray to the ends.
The deeper friend cast me off for a man.
That friendship—like what to wear when
   hurried

by one's schedule, the satisfying skirt
one grabs, for it fits and fits till it bags—hurt
not to fix. Ditching loved clothes hurts because
all age does; holes like mouths sag open: *it was.*

—*Molly Peacock*

A PLACE FOR YOU
BY MY SIDE ⌒⌒

The Meeting

After so long an absence
At last we meet again;
Does the meeting give us pleasure
Or does it give us pain?

The tree of life has been shaken,
And but few of us linger now,
Like the prophet's two or three berries
In the top of the uppermost bough.

We cordially greet each other
In the old familiar tone;
And we think, though we do not say it,
How old and gray he is grown!

We speak of a Merry Christmas,
And many a happy New Year;
But each in his heart is thinking
Of those that are not here.

We speak of friends and their fortunes,
And of what they did and said,
Till the dead alone seem living,
And the living alone seem dead.

And at last we hardly distinguish
Between the ghosts and the guests;
And a mist and shadow of sadness
Steals over our merriest jests.

—*Henry Wadsworth Longfellow*

A Wayfaring Song

O who will walk a mile with me
   Along life's merry way?
A comrade blithe and full of glee,
Who dares to laugh out loud and free
And let his frolic fancy play,
Like a happy child, through the flowers gay
That fill the field and fringe the way
   Where he walks a mile with me.

And who will walk a mile with me
   Along life's weary way?
A friend whose heart has eyes to see
The stars shine out o'er the darkening lea,
And the quiet rest at the end o' the day,—
A friend who knows, and dares to say,
The brave, sweet words that cheer the way
   Where he walks a mile with me.

With such a comrade, such a friend,
I fain would walk till journey's end,
Through summer sunshine, winter rain,
And then?—Farewell, we shall meet again!

—*Henry van Dyke*

Happiness

So early it's still almost dark out.
I'm near the window with coffee,
and the usual early morning stuff
that passes for thought.
When I see the boy and his friend
walking up the road
to deliver the newspaper.
They wear caps and sweaters,
and one boy has a bag over his shoulder.
They are so happy
they aren't saying anything, these boys.
I think if they could, they would take
each other's arm.
It's early in the morning,
and they are doing this thing together.
They come on, slowly.
The sky is taking on light,
though the moon still hangs pale over the water.

Such beauty that for a minute
death and ambition, even love,
doesn't enter into this.
Happiness. It comes on
unexpectedly. And goes beyond, really,
any early morning talk about it.

—*Raymond Carver*

The Morning Walk

When Anne and I go out a walk,
We hold each other's hand and talk
Of all the things we mean to do
When Anne and I are forty-two.

And when we've thought about a thing,
Like bowling hoops or bicycling,
Or falling down on Anne's balloon,
We do it in the afternoon.

—*A. A. Milne*

Sitting at Night

A quiet valley with no man's footprints,
An empty garden lit by the moon.
Suddenly my dog barks and I know
A friend with a bottle is knocking at the gate.

—Ŏm Ŭi-gil

Translated from the Chinese by Kim Jong-Gil

There Is Always a Place For You

There is always a place for you at my table,
 You never need be invited.
I'll share every crust as long as I'm able,
 And know you will be delighted.
There is always a place for you by my fire,
 And though it may burn to embers,
If warmth and good cheer are your desire
 The friend of your heart remembers!
There is always a place for you by my side,
 And should the years tear us apart,
I will face lonely moments more satisfied
 With a place for you in my heart!

—*Anne Campbell*

Inviting a Friend to Supper

Tonight, grave sir, both my poor house, and I
Do equally desire your company:
Not that we think us worthy such a guest,
But that your worth will dignify our feast,
With those that come; whose grace may make
   that seem
Something, which, else, could hope for no
   esteem.
It is the fair acceptance, sir, creates
The entertainment perfect: not the cates.
Yet shall you have, to rectify your palate,
An olive, capers, or some better salad
Ush'ring the mutton; with a short-legged hen,
If we can get her, full of eggs, and then,
Lemons, and wine for sauce: to these, a cony
Is not to be despaired of, for our money;
And, though fowl, now, be scarce, yet there are
   clerks,
The sky not falling, think we may have larks.
I'll tell you of more, and lie, so you will come:

Of partridge, pheasant, woodcock, of which
    some
May yet be there; and godwit, if we can:
Knat, rail, and ruff too. Howso e'er, my man
Shall read a piece of Virgil, Tacitus,
Livy, or of some better book to us,
Of which we'll speak our minds, amidst our
    meat;
And I'll profess no verses to repeat:
To this, if aught appear, which I not know of,
That will the pastry, not my paper, show of.
Digestive cheese, and fruit there sure will be;
But that, which most doth take my Muse,
    and me,
Is a pure cup of rich canary wine,
Which is the Mermaid's, now, but shall be mine:
Of which had Horace, or Anacreon tasted,
Their lives, as do their lines, till now had lasted.
Tobacco, nectar, or the Thespian spring,
Are all but Luther's beer, to this I sing.

Of this we will sup free, but moderately,
And we will have no Pooly, or Parrot by;
Nor shall our cups make any guilty men:
But, at our parting, we will be, as when
We innocently met. No simple word,
That shall be uttered at our mirthful board,
Shall make us sad next morning: or affright
The liberty, that we'll enjoy tonight.

—*Ben Jonson*

Inviting Guests

I sent out invitations
To summon guests.
I collected together
All my friends.
Loud talk
And simple feasting:
Discussion of philosophy,
Investigation of subtleties.
Tongues loosened
And minds at one.
Hearts refreshed
By discharge of emotion!

—*Ch'eng-Kung Sui*

The Royal Guest

They tell me I am shrewd with other men;
  With thee I'm slow, and difficult of speech.
With others I may guide the car of talk;
  Thou wing'st it oft to realms beyond my
      reach.

If other guests should come, I'd deck my hair,
  And choose my newest garment from the
      shelf;
When thou art bidden, I would clothe my heart
  With holiest purpose, as for God himself.

For them I while the hours with tale or song,
  Or web of fancy, fringed with careless rhyme;
But how to find a fitting lay for thee,
  Who hast the harmonies of every time?

O friend beloved! I sit apart and dumb,—
  Sometimes in sorrow, oft in joy divine;
My lip will falter, but my prisoned heart
  Springs forth to measure its faint pulse with
    thine.

Thou art to me like a royal guest,
  Whose travels bring him to some lowly roof,
Where simple rustics spread their festal fare
  And, blushing, own it is not good enough.

Bethink thee, then, whene'er thou com'st to me,
  From high emprise and noble toil to rest,
My thoughts are weak and trivial, matched
    with thine;
  But the poor mansion offers thee its best.

—*Julia Ward Howe*

For Friends Only

(for John and Teckla Clark)

Ours yet not ours, being set apart
As a shrine to friendship,
Empty and silent most of the year,
This room awaits from you
What you alone, as visitor, can bring,
A week-end of personal life.

In a house backed by orderly woods,
Facing a tractored sugar-beet country,
Your working hosts engaged to their stint,
You are unlike to encounter
Dragons or romance: were drama a craving,
You would not have come.

Books we do have for almost any
Literate mood, and notepaper, envelopes,
For a writing one (to "borrow" stamps
Is the mark of ill-breeding):
Between lunch and tea, perhaps a drive;
After dinner, music or gossip.

Should you have troubles (pets will die
Lovers are always behaving badly)
And confession helps, we will hear it,
Examine and give our counsel:
If to mention them hurts too much,
We shall not be nosey.

Easy at first, the language of friendship
Is, as we soon discover,
Very difficult to speak well, a tongue
With no cognates, no resemblance
To the galimatias of nursery and bedroom,
Court rhyme or shepherd's prose,

And, unless spoken often, soon goes rusty.
Distance and duties divide us,
But absence will not seem an evil
If it make our re-meeting
A real occasion. Come when you can:
Your room will be ready.

In Tum-Tum's reign a tin of biscuits
On the bedside table provided
For nocturnal munching. Now weapons have
   changed,
And the fashion of appetites:
There, for sunbathers who count their calories,
A bottle of mineral water.

Felicissima notte! May you fall at once
Into a cordial dream, assured
That whoever slept in this bed before
Was also someone we like,
That within the circle of our affection
Also you have no double.

—*W. H. Auden*

REMEMBRANCE OF
THINGS PAST

Auld Lang Syne

Should auld acquaintance be forgot,
And never brought to mind?
Should auld acquaintance be forgot,
And days o' lang syne?

> *For auld lang syne, my dear*
> *For auld lang syne,*
> *We'll take a cup o' kindness yet*
> *For auld lang syne.*

—*Robert Burns*

Friends of Youth

The half-seen memories of childish days,
When pains and pleasures lightly came and
   went;
The sympathies of boyhood rashly spent
In fearful wanderings through forbidden ways;
The vague, but manly wish to tread the maze
Of life to noble ends,—whereon intent,
Asking to know for what man here is sent,
The bravest heart must often pause and gaze;
The firm resolve to seek the chosen end
Of manhood's judgment, cautious and
   mature,—
Each of these viewless bonds binds friend to
   friend
With strength no selfish purpose can secure:
My happy lot is this, that all attend
That friendship which first came and which
   shall last endure.

—*Aubrey Thomas de Vere*

Sonnet 30

When to the sessions of sweet silent thought
I summon up remembrance of things past,
I sigh the lack of many a thing I sought,
And with old woes new wail my dear times'
    waste:
Then can I drown an eye, unus'd to flow,
For precious friends hid in death's dateless night,
And weep afresh love's long since cancell'd woe,
And moan the expense of many a vanish'd sight:
Then can I grieve at grievances foregone,
And heavily from woe to woe tell o'er
The sad account of fore-bemoaned moan,
Which I new pay as if not paid before.
  But if the while I think on thee, dear friend,
  All losses are restor'd and sorrows end.

—*William Shakespeare*

Filling in the
New Address Book

But rifling through the old one,
choosing whom to preserve
in your encyclopedia of associates,
whom to let become obsolete—
no room for them in your entire world.
You little god, you,
you puny pocket of omnipotence—
how you throw people off the side
of your dinghy-book,
a tiny captain thinking, "This is dead weight."
Old girlfriends—doubly gone now.
Old drinking buddies, married and laden
with responsibility, that grand soberer.
So you continue, you infinitesimal infinite one,
scratching out the names of the dead,
people you are coming from and never toward,
tearing down street signs, phone lines,

upheaving entire highways between you
as you leave them out,
their new and unfamiliar lives
not any less full than if you included them.
They are manning their own ships and,
sorry little god,
no room for you on their voyage either.
It's understood, no? You've been heroes together
in the past lives within this life—
Ulysseses now full of uselessnesses—
and why threaten any miraculous history,
any great testament, with knowledge
of how empty your current book of stories is?

—*B. J. Ward*

Dreaming That I Went with Li and Yü to Visit Yüan Chēn

(Written in exile)

At night I dreamt I was back in Ch'ang-an;
I saw again the faces of old friends.
And in my dreams, under an April sky,
They led me by the hand to wander in the
    spring winds.
Together we came to the village of Peace and
    Quiet;
We stopped our horses at the gate of Yüan
    Chēn.
Yüan Chēn was sitting all alone;
When he saw me coming, a smile came to his
    face.
He pointed back at the flowers in the western
    court;
Then opened the wine in the northern
    summer-house.
He seemed to be saying that neither of us had
    changed;

He seemed to be regretting that joy will not
    stay;
That our souls had met only for a little while,
To part again with hardly time for greeting.
I woke up and thought him still at my side;
I put out my hand; there was nothing there
    at all.

—*Po Chü-i*
Translated from the Chinese by Arthur Waley

Paying Calls

I went by footpath and by stile
Beyond where bustle ends,
Strayed here a mile and there a mile
And called upon some friends.

On certain ones I had not seen
For years past did I call,
And then on others who had been
The oldest friends of all.

It was the time of midsummer
When they had used to roam;
But now, though tempting was the air,
I found them all at home.

I spoke to one and other of them
By mound and stone and tree
Of things we had done ere days were dim,
But they spoke not to me.

—*Thomas Hardy*

Bill and Joe

Come, dear old comrade, you and I
Will steal an hour from days gone by,
The shining days when life was new,
And all was bright with morning dew,
The lusty days of long ago,
When you were Bill and I was Joe.

Your name may flaunt a titled trail
Proud as a cockerel's rainbow tail,
And mine as brief appendix wear
As Tam O'Shanter's luckless mare;
To-day, old friend, remember still
That I am Joe and you are Bill.

You've won the great world's envied prize,
And grand you look in people's eyes,
With HON. and LL.D.
In big brave letters, fair to see,—
Your fist, old fellow! off they go!—
How are you, Bill? How are you, Joe?

You've worn the judge's ermined robe;
You've taught your name to half the globe;
You've sung mankind a deathless strain;
You've made the dead past live again:
The world may call you what it will,
But you and I are Joe and Bill.

The chaffing young folks stare and say
"See those old buffers, bent and gray,—
They talk like fellows in their teens!
Mad, poor old boys! That's what it means,"—
And shake their heads; they little know
The throbbing hearts of Bill and Joe!—

How Bill forgets his hour of pride,
While Joe sits smiling at his side;
How Joe, in spite of time's disguise,
Finds the old schoolmate in his eyes,—
Those calm, stern eyes that melt and fill
As Joe looks fondly up at Bill.

Ah, pensive scholar, what is fame?
A fitful tongue of leaping flame;
A giddy whirlwind's fickle gust,
That lifts a pinch of mortal dust;
A few swift years, and who can show
Which dust was Bill and which was Joe?

The weary idol takes his stand,
Holds out his bruised and aching hand,
While gaping thousands come and go,—
How vain it seems, this empty show!
Till all at once his pulses thrill;—
'Tis poor old Joe's "God bless you, Bill!"

And shall we breathe in happier spheres
The names that pleased our mortal ears;
In some sweet lull of harp and song
For earth-born spirits none too long,
Just whispering of the world below
Where this was Bill, and that was Joe?

No matter; while our home is here
No sounding name is half so dear;
When fades at length our lingering day,
Who cares what pompous tombstones say?
Read on the hearts that love us still,
Hic jacet Joe. *Hic jacet* Bill.

—*Oliver Wendell Holmes*

Old Times

Friend of my youth, let us talk of old times;
Of the long lost golden hours.
When "Winter" meant only Christmas chimes,
And "Summer" wreaths of flowers.
Life has grown old, and cold, my friend,
And the winter now, means death.
And summer blossoms speak all too plain
Of the dear, dead forms beneath.

But let us talk of the past to-night;
And live it over again,
We will put the long years out of sight,
And dream we are young as then.
But you must not look at me, my friend,
And I must not look at you,
Or the furrowed brows, and silvered locks,
Will prove our dream untrue.

Let us sing of the summer, too sweet to last,
And yet too sweet to die.
Let us read tales, from the book of the past,
And talk of the days gone by.
We will turn our backs to the West, my friend,
And forget we are growing old.
The skies of the Present are dull, and gray,
But the Past's are blue, and gold.

The sun has passed over the noontide line
And is sinking down the West.
And of friends we knew in days Lang Syne,
Full half have gone to rest.
And the few that are left on earth, my friend
Are scattered far, and wide.
But you and I will talk of the days
Ere any roamed, or died.

Auburn ringlets, and hazel eyes
Blue eyes and tresses of gold.
Winds joy laden, and azure skies,
Belong to those days of old.
We will leave the Present's shores awhile
And float on the Past's smooth sea.
But I must not look at you, my friend,
And you must not look at me.

—*Ella Wheeler Wilcox*

Old Chums

Is it you, Jack? Old boy, is it really you?
  I shouldn't have known you but that I was told
You might be expected;—pray how do you do?
  But what, under heaven, has made you so old?

Your hair! why, you've only a little gray fuzz!
  And your beard's white! but that can be
    beautifully dyed;
And your legs aren't but just half as long as
    they was;
  And then—stars and garters! your vest is so
    wide!

Is that your hand? Lord, how I envied you that
  In the time of our courting,—so soft and so
    small,
And now it is callous inside, and so fat,—
  Well, you beat the very old deuce, that is all.

Turn round! let me look at you! isn't it odd,
  How strange in a few years a fellow's chum
    grows!
Your eye is shrunk up like a bean in a pod,
  And what are these lines branching out from
    your nose?

Your back has gone up and your shoulders
    gone down,
  And all the old roses are under the plough;
Why, Jack, if we'd happened to meet about town,
  I wouldn't have known you from Adam, I vow!

You've had trouble, have you? I'm sorry; but
    John,
  All trouble sits lightly at your time of life.
How's Billy, my namesake? You don't say he's
    gone
  To the war, John, and that you have buried
    your wife?

Poor Katharine! so she has left you—ah me!
 I thought she would live to be fifty, or more.
What is it you tell me? She was fifty-three!
 Oh no, Jack! she wasn't so much, by a score!

Well, there's little Katy,—was that her name,
  John?
 She'll rule your house one of these days like a
  queen.
That baby! good Lord! is she married and
  gone?
 With a Jack ten years old! and a Katy
  fourteen!

Then I give it up! Why, you're younger than I
 By ten or twelve years, and to think you've
  come back
A sober old graybeard, just ready to die!
 I don't understand how it is—do you, Jack?

I've got all my faculties yet, sound and bright;
   Slight failure my eyes are beginning to hint;
But still, with my spectacles on, and a light
   'Twixt them and the page, I can read any
      print.

My hearing is dull, and my leg is more spare,
   Perhaps, than it was when I beat you at ball;
My breath gives out, too, if I go up a stair,—
   But nothing worth mentioning, nothing at all!

My hair is just turning a little you see,
   And lately I've put on a broader-brimmed hat
Than I wore at your wedding, but you will
      agree,
   Old fellow, I look all the better for that.

I'm sometimes a little rheumatic, 'tis true,
  And my nose isn't quite on a straight line,
    they say;
For all that, I don't think I've changed much,
    do you?
  And I don't feel a day older, Jack, not a day.

—*Alice Cary*

The Arrow and the Song

I shot an arrow into the air,
It fell to earth, I knew not where;
For, so swiftly it flew, the sight
Could not follow it in its flight.

I breathed a song into the air,
It fell to earth, I knew not where;
For who has sight so keen and strong,
That it can follow the flight of song?

Long, long afterward, in an oak
I found the arrow, still unbroke;
And the song, from beginning to end,
I found again in the heart of a friend.

—*Henry Wadsworth Longfellow*

ONE FRIEND TO
ANOTHER ⟿

To a Friend

You entered my life in a casual way,
   And saw at a glance what I needed;
There were others who passed me or met me
     each day,
   But never a one of them heeded.
Perhaps you were thinking of other folks more,
   Or chance simply seemed to decree it;
I know there were many such chances before,
   But the others—well, they didn't see it.

You said just the thing that I wished you would
     say,
   And you made me believe that you meant it;
I held up my head in the old gallant way,
   And resolved you should never repent it.
There are times when encouragement means
     such a lot,
   And a word is enough to convey it;
There were others who could have, as easy as
     not—
   But, just the same, they didn't say it.

There may have been someone who could have
    done more
  To help me along, though I doubt it;
What I needed was cheering, and always before
  They had let me plod onward without it.
You helped to refashion the dream of my heart,
  And made me turn eagerly to it;
There were others who might have (I question
    that part)—
  But, after all, they didn't do it!

—*Grace Stricker Dawson*

The Lover Pleads with His Friend for Old Friends

Though you are in your shining days,
Voices among the crowd
And new friends busy with your praise,
Be not unkind or proud,
But think about old friends the most:
Time's bitter flood will rise,
Your beauty perish and be lost
For all eyes but these eyes.

—*William Butler Yeats*

Friendship

O friend, we sit together, and the room
Seems wonder-filled with love and trembling
    youth,
And in its beauty we have pledged our hearts
      To unity.
We pledge our loyalty, our honor and our truth
In the old, old words of an eternity.

And yet I know that we must part, and then
My way and thine, wide-circling wander far.
I still may pledge my honor to a star—
But thou art lost, and I to thee
In the fitful loneliness of memory
      Return again.

O friend, I have no other claim on thee
Save that thou and I together spent
      Some happy hours.

We cannot bind
The wilful waywardness of mortal mind,
But only dream in golden-crowned content
    Of the springtime flowers.

O friend, when thou and I are far apart
In the rough-hewn bypaths of the is-to-be,
I bid thee when our friendship chills thy heart
And lies a cold dead body when thou wouldst
    be free,—
Or, like a bird, in trembling restlessness
Would try its wings in yet one final test,—
I bid thee open thy soul and give it liberty.

—*Dorothy Grafly*

Sonnet 263

To me, fair friend, you never can be old,
For as you were when first your eye I eyed,
Such seems your beauty still: Three winters
 cold,
Have from the forests shook three summers'
 pride;
Three beauteous springs to yellow autumn
 turned,
In process of the seasons have I seen,
Three April perfumes in three hot Junes burned,
Since first I saw you fresh which yet are green.
Ah! yet doth beauty, like a dial-hand,
Steal from his figure, and no pace perceived;
So your sweet hue, which methinks still doth
 stand,
Hath motion, and mine eye may be deceived.
 For fear of which, hear this, thou age unbred,
 Ere you were born was beauty's summer dead.

—*William Shakespeare*

To Richard Watson Gilder

Old friends are best! And so to you
Again I send, in closer throng,
No unfamiliar shapes of song,
But those that once you liked and knew.

You surely will not do them wrong;
For are you not an old friend, too?—
         Old friends are best.

Old books, old wine, old Nankin blue;—
All things, in short, to which belong
The charm, the grace that Time makes strong,—
All these I prize, but (*entre nous*)
         Old friends are best!

—*Henry Austin Dobson*

My Old Friend

You've a manner all so mellow,
My old friend,
That it cheers and warms a fellow,
My old friend,
Just to meet and greet you, and
Feel the pressure of a hand
That one may understand,
My old friend.

Though dimmed in youthful splendor,
My old friend,
Your smiles are still as tender,
My old friend,
And your eyes as true a blue
As your childhood ever knew,
And your laugh as merry, too,
My old friend.

For though your hair is faded,
My old friend,
And your step a trifle jaded,
My old friend,
Old Time, with all his lures
In the trophies he secures,
Leaves young that heart of yours,
My old friend.

And so it is you cheer me,
My old friend,
For to know you and be near you,
My old friend,
Makes my hopes of clearer light,
And my faith of surer sight,
And my soul a purer white,
My old friend.

—*James Whitcomb Riley*

My Friend, The Things That Do Attain

My friend, the things that do attain
   The happy life be these, I find:
The riches left, not got with pain;
   The fruitful ground; the quiet mind;

The equal friend; no grudge; no strife;
   No charge of rule, nor governance;
Without disease, the healthy life;
   The household of continuance;

The mean diet, no dainty fare;
   Wisdom joined with simpleness;
The night discharged of all care,
   Where wine the wit may not oppress:

The faithful wife, without debate;
   Such sleeps as may beguile the night;
Content thyself with thine estate,
   Neither wish death, nor fear his might.

—*Henry Howard, Earl of Surrey*

Friendship

When we were idlers with the loitering rills,
The need of human love we little noted:
  Our love was nature; and the peace that floated
On the white mist, and dwelt upon the hills,
To sweet accord subdued our wayward wills:
  One soul was ours, one mind, one heart
      devoted,
  That, wisely doting, ask'd not why it doted,
And ours the unknown joy, which knowing kills.
But now I find how dear thou wert to me;
  That man is more than half of nature's
      treasure,
Of that fair beauty which no eye can see,
  Of that sweet music which no ear can measure;
  And now the streams may sing for others'
      pleasure,
The hills sleep on in their eternity.

—*Hartley Coleridge*

To a Friend

I ask but one thing of you, only one,
    That always you will be my dream of you;
    That never shall I wake to find untrue
All this I have believed and rested on,
Forever vanished, like a vision gone
    Out into the night. Alas, how few
    There are who strike in us a chord we knew
Existed, but so seldom heard its tone
    We tremble at the half-forgotten sound.
The world is full of rude awakenings
    And heaven-born castles shattered to the
        ground,
Yet still our human longing vainly clings
    To a belief in beauty through all wrongs.
    O stay your hand, and leave my heart its songs!

—*Amy Lowell*

Friendship

O friend, my bosom said,
Through thee alone the sky is arched,
Through thee the rose is red;
All things through thee take nobler form,
And look beyond the earth;
The mill-round of our fate appears
A sun-path in thy worth.
Me too thy nobleness has taught
To master my despair;
The fountains of my hidden life,
Are through thy friendship fair.

—*Ralph Waldo Emerson*

If I Had Known

If I had known what trouble you were bearing;
What griefs were in the silence of your face;
I would have been more gentle, and more caring,
And tried to give you gladness for a space.
I would have brought more warmth into the
    place,
  If I had known.
If I had known what thoughts despairing drew
    you;
(Why do we never try to understand?)
I would have lent a little friendship to you,
And slipped my hand within your hand,
And made your stay more pleasant in the land,
  If I had known.

—*Mary Carolyn Davies*

Accept My Full Heart's Thanks

Your words came just when needed.
Like a breeze,
Blowing and bringing from the wide salt sea
Some cooling spray, to meadow scorched with
   heat
And choked with dust and clouds of sifted sand
That hateful whirlwinds, envious of its bloom,
Had tossed upon it. But the cool sea breeze
Came laden with the odors of the sea
And damp with spray, that laid the dust and sand
And brought new life and strength to blade and
   bloom
So words of thine came over miles to me,
Fresh from the mighty sea, a true friend's heart,
And brought me hope, and strength, and swept
   away
The dusty webs that human spiders spun
Across my path. Friend—and the word means
   much—

So few there are who reach like thee, a hand
Up over all the barking curs of spite
And give the clasp, when most its need is felt,
Friend, newly found, accept my full heart's
    thanks.

—*Ella Wheeler Wilcox*

To a Friend

We parted on the mountains, as two streams
From one clear spring pursue their several ways;
And thy fleet course hath been through many a
    maze
In foreign lands, where silvery Padus gleams
To that delicious sky, whose glowing beams
Brighten'd the tresses that old poets praise;
Where Petrarch's patient love, and artful lays,
And Ariosto's song of many themes,
Moved the soft air. But I, a lazy brook,
As close pent up within my native dell,
Have crept along from nook to shady nook,
Where flow'rets blow, and whispering Naiads
    dwell.
Yet now we meet, that parted were so wide,
O'er rough and smooth to travel side by side.

—*Hartley Coleridge*

I Read, Dear Friend

I read, dear friend, in your dear face
Your life's tale told with perfect grace;
The river of your life, I trace
Up the sun-chequered, devious bed
To the far-distant fountain-head.

Not one quick beat of your warm heart,
Nor thought that came to you apart,
Pleasure nor pity, love nor pain
Nor sorrow, has gone by in vain;

But as some lone, wood-wandering child
Brings home with him at evening mild
The thorns and flowers of all the wild,
From your whole life, O fair and true
Your flowers and thorns you bring with you!

—*Robert Louis Stevenson*

JUST GOOD FRIENDS

Platonic

I knew it the first of the Summer—
I knew it the same at the end—
That you and your love were plighted,
But couldn't you be my friend?
Couldn't we sit in the twilight,
Couldn't we walk on the shore,
With only a pleasant friendship
To bind us, and nothing more?

There was not a word of nonsense
Spoken between us two,
Though we lingered oft in the garden
Till the roses were wet with dew.
We touched on a thousand subjects—
The moon and the worlds above;
But our talk was tinctured with science,
With never a hint of love.

"A wholly Platonic friendship,"
You said I had proved to you,
"Could bind a man and a woman
The whole long season through,
With never a thought of folly,
Though both are in their youth."
What would you have said, my lady,
If you had known the truth?

Had I done what my mad heart prompted—
Gone down on my knees to you,
And told you my passionate story
There in the dusk and dew;
My burning, burdensome story,
Hidden and hushed so long,
My story of hopeless loving—
Say, would you have thought it wrong?

But I fought with my heart and conquered;
I hid my wound from sight;
You were going away in the morning,
And I said a calm good-night.
But now, when I sit in the twilight,
Or when I walk by the sea
That friendship, quite "platonic"
Comes surging over me.
And a passionate longing fills me
For the roses, the dusk and the dew,—
For the beautiful Summer vanished—
For the moonlight talks—and you.

—*Ella Wheeler Wilcox*

Lines to an Old Sweetheart

Once fondly lov'd, and still remember'd dear,
   Sweet early Object of my youthful vows,
Accept this mark of friendship, warm, sincere,
   Friendship—'tis all cold duty now allows.

And while you read the simple, artless rhymes,
   One friendly sigh for him—he asks no more,
Who, distant, burns in flaming torrid climes,
   Or haply lies beneath th' Atlantic roar.

—*Robert Burns*

Friend and Lover

When Psyche's friend becomes her lover,
How sweetly these conditions blend!
But, oh, what anguish to discover
Her lover has become—her friend!

—*Mary Ainge de Vere*

Promises Like a Pie-Crust

Promise me no promises,
　So will I not promise you;
Keep we both our liberties,
　Never false and never true:
Let us hold the die uncast,
　Free to come as free to go;
For I cannot know your past,
　And of mine what can you know?

You, so warm, may once have been
　Warmer towards another one;
I, so cold, may once have seen
　Sunlight, once have felt the sun:
Who shall show us if it was
　Thus indeed in time of old?
Fades the image from the glass
　And the fortune is not told.

If you promised, you might grieve
   For lost liberty again;
If I promised, I believe
   I should fret to break the chain:
Let us be the friends we were,
   Nothing more but nothing less;
Many thrive on frugal fare
   Who would perish of excess.

—*Christina Georgina Rossetti*

Being Her Friend

Being her friend, I do not care, not I,
　　How gods or men may wrong me, beat me
　　　　down;
Her word's sufficient star to travel by,
　　I count her quiet praise sufficient crown.

Being her friend, I do not covet gold,
　　Save for a royal gift to give her pleasure;
To sit with her, and have her hand to hold,
　　Is wealth, I think, surpassing minted treasure.

Being her friend, I only covet art,
　　A white pure flame to search me as I trace
In crooked letters from a throbbing heart
　　The hymn to beauty written on her face.

—John Masefield

Love and Friendship

Love is like the wild rose-briar;
  Friendship like the holly-tree.
The holly is dark when the rose-briar blooms,
  But which will bloom most constantly?

The wild rose-briar is sweet in spring,
  Its summer blossoms scent the air;
Yet wait till winter comes again,
  And who will call the wild-briar fair?

Then, scorn the silly rose-wreath now,
  And deck thee with holly's sheen,
That, when December blights thy brow,
  He still may leave thy garland green.

—*Emily Brontë*

We Talk of Taxes, and I Call You Friend

We talk of taxes, and I call you friend;
Well, such you are,—but well enough we know
How thick about us root, how rankly grow
Those subtle weeds no man has need to tend,
That flourish through neglect, and soon must
    send
Perfume too sweet upon us and overthrow
Our steady senses; how such matters go
We are aware, and how such matters end.
Yet shall be told no meagre passion here;
With lovers such as we forevermore
Isolde drinks the draught, and Guinevere
Receives the Table's ruin through her door,
Francesca, with the loud surf at her ear,
Lets fall the colored book upon the floor.

—*Edna St. Vincent Millay*

The Heart's Friend

Fair is the white star of twilight,
   and the sky clearer
At the day's end;
But she is fairer, and she is dearer.
She, my heart's friend!

Far stars and fair in the skies bending,
Low stars of hearth fires and wood smoke
   ascending,
The meadow-lark's nested,
The night hawk is winging;
Home through the star-shine the hunter comes
   singing.

Fair is the white star of twilight,
And the moon roving
To the sky's end;
But she is fairer, better worth loving,
She, my heart's friend.

—*A Shoshone Love Song*

Friendship after Love

After the fierce midsummer all ablaze
  Has burned itself to ashes, and expires
  In the intensity of its own fires,
There come the mellow, mild, St. Martin days
Crowned with the calm of peace, but sad with
    haze.
  So after love has led us, till he tires
  Of his own throes, and torments, and desires,
Comes large-eyed friendship: with a restful gaze,
He beckons us to follow, and across
  Cool verdant vales we wander free from care.
  Is it a touch of frost lies in the air?
Why are we haunted with a sense of loss?
We do not wish the pain back, or the heat;
And yet, and yet, these days are incomplete.

—*Ella Wheeler Wilcox*

The Lost Mistress

All's over, then: does truth sound bitter
   As one at first believes?
Hark, 'tis the sparrows' good-night twitter
   About your cottage eaves!

And the leaf-buds on the vine are woolly,
   I noticed that, to-day;
One day more bursts them open fully
   —You know the red turns gray.

To-morrow we meet the same then, dearest?
   May I take your hand in mine?
Mere friends are we, —well, friends the merest
   Keep much that I resign:

For each glance of the eye so bright and black,
   Though I keep with heart's endeavor, —
Your voice, when you wish the snowdrops back,
   Though it stay in my soul forever! —

Yet I will but say what mere friends say,
   Or only a thought stronger;
I will hold your hand but as long as all may,
   Or so very little longer!

—*Robert Browning*

FRIENDS WITH FUR
AND FEATHERS ～

Lux, My Fair Falcon

Lux, my fair falcon, and your fellows all,
  How well pleasaunt it were your liberty!
Ye not forsake me that fair might ye befall.
  But they that sometime lik'd my company,
Like lice away from dead bodies they crawl.
  Lo, what a proof in light adversity!
But ye, my birds, I swear by all your bells,
Ye be my friends, and so be but few else.

—*Sir Thomas Wyatt*

Three

We were just three,
Two loons and me.
They swam and fished,
I watched and wished,
That I, like them might dive and play
In icy waters all the day.
I watch and wished. I could not reach
Where they were, till I tried their speech,
And something in me helped, so I
Could give their trembling sort of cry.
One loon looked up and answered me.
He understood that we were three.

—*Elizabeth Coatsworth*

To Flush, My Dog

I

Loving friend, the gift of one
Who her own true faith has run
    Through thy lower nature,
Be my benediction said
With my hand upon thy head,
    Gentle fellow-creature!

II

Like a lady's ringlets brown,
Flow thy silken ears adown
    Either side demurely
Of thy silver-suited breast
Shining out from all the rest
    Of thy body purely.

III

Darkly brown thy body is,
Till the sunshine striking this
    Alchemize its dulness,

When the sleek curls manifold
Flash all over into gold
  With a burnished fulness.

IV

Underneath my stroking hand,
Startled eyes of hazel bland
  Kindling, growing larger,
Up thou leapest with a spring,
Full of prank and curveting,
  Leaping like a charger.

V

Leap! thy broad tail waves a light,
Leap! thy slender feet are bright,
  Canopied in fringes;
Leap! those tasselled ears of thine
Flicker strangely, fair and fine
  Down their golden inches.

VI

Yet, my pretty, sportive friend,
Little is't to such an end
    That I praise thy rareness;
Other dogs may be thy peers
Haply in these drooping ears
    And this glossy fairness.

VII

But of *thee* it shall be said,
This dog watched beside a bed
    Day and night unweary,
Watched within a curtained room
Where no sunbeam brake the gloom
    Round the sick and dreary.

VIII

Roses, gathered for a vase,
In that chamber died apace,
    Beam and breeze resigning;

This dog only, waited on,
Knowing that when light is gone
  Love remains for shining.

IX
Other dogs in thymy dew
Tracked the hares and followed through
  Sunny moor or meadow;
This dog only, crept and crept
Next a languid cheek that slept,
  Sharing in the shadow.

X
Other dogs of loyal cheer
Bounded at the whistle clear,
  Up the woodside hieing;
This dog only, watched in reach
Of a faintly uttered speech
  Or a louder sighing.

XI

And if one or two quick tears
Dropped upon his glossy ears
   Or a sigh came double,
Up he sprang in eager haste,
Fawning, fondling, breathing fast,
   In a tender trouble.

XII

And this dog was satisfied
If a pale thin hand would glide
   Down his dewlaps sloping,—
Which he pushed his nose within,
After,—platforming his chin
   On the palm left open.

XIII

This dog, if a friendly voice
Call him now to blither choice
   Than such chamber-keeping,
'Come out!' praying from the door,—
Presseth backward as before,
   Up against me leaping.

XIV

Therefore to this dog will I,
Tenderly not scornfully,
   Render praise and favor:
With my hand upon his head,
Is my benediction said
   Therefore and for ever.

XV

And because he loves me so,
Better than his kind will do
   Often man or woman,
Give I back more love again
Than dogs often take of men,
   Leaning from my Human.

XVI

Blessings on thee, dog of mine,
Pretty collars make thee fine,
   Sugared milk make fat thee!
Pleasures wag on in thy tail,
Hands of gentle motion fail
   Nevermore, to pat thee!

XVII

Downy pillow take thy head,
Silken coverlid bestead,
   Sunshine help thy sleeping!
No fly's buzzing wake thee up,
No man break thy purple cup
   Set for drinking deep in.

XVIII

Whiskered cats arointed flee,
Sturdy stoppers keep from thee
   Cologne distillations;
Nuts lie in thy path for stones,
And thy feast-day macaroons
   Turn to daily rations!

XIX

Mock I thee, in wishing weal?—
Tears are in my eyes to feel
   Thou art made so straitly,
Blessing needs must straiten too,—
Little canst thou joy or do,
   Thou who lovest *greatly.*

XX

Yet be blessed to the height
Of all good and all delight
   Pervious to thy nature;
Only *loved* beyond that line,
With a love that answers thine,
   Loving fellow-creature!

—*Elizabeth Barrett Browning*

Chums

He sits and begs, he gives a paw.
He is, as you can see,
The finest dog you ever saw,
And he belongs to me.

He follows everywhere I go
And even when I swim.
I laugh because he thinks, you know,
That I belong to him.

But still, no matter what we do
We never have a fuss;
And so, I guess, it must be true
That we belong to us.

—*Arthur Guiterman*

Making Friends

The eve I came the dog 'gan bark;
The two cats, every hair made stark,
Hid 'neath the clock; the baby woke,
And into shrieks of terror broke;
The Dame glanced angrily the while:
Now when I come she grants a smile;
The babe crows to me from its bed;
The dog upon my knees its head
Places; the cats lie on my feet,
And thus their friend all friendly greet.

—*Julien Auguste Pelage Brizeux*
Translated from the French by Henry Carrington

An Epitaph

His friends he loved. His direst earthly foes—
   Cats—I believe he did but feign to hate.
My hand will miss the insinuated nose,
   Mine eyes the tail that wagg'd contempt at
      Fate.

—*William Watson*

The Monk and His White Cat

Pangar, my white cat, and I
   Silent ply our special crafts;
Hunting mice his one pursuit,
   Mine to shoot keen spirit shafts.

Rest I love, all fame beyond,
   In the bond of some rare book;
Yet white Pangar from his play
   Casts, my way, no jealous look.

Thus alone within one cell
   Safe we dwell—not dull the tale—
Since his ever favourite sport
   Each to court will never fail.

Now a mouse, to swell his spoils,
   In his toils he spears with skill;
Now a meaning deeply thought
   I have caught with startled thrill.

Now his green full-shining gaze
    Darts its rays against the wall;
Now my feebler glances mark
    Through the dark bright knowledge fall.

Leaping up with joyful purr,
    In mouse fur his sharp claw sticks,
Problems difficult and dear
    With my spear I, too, transfix.

Crossing not each other's will,
    Diverse still, yet still allied,
Following each his own lone ends,
    Constant friends we here abide.

Pangar, master of his art,
    Plays his part in pranksome youth;
While, in age sedate, I clear
    Shadows from the sphere of Truth.

—*Anonymous*

Last Words to a Dumb Friend

Pet was never mourned as you,
Purrer of the spotless hue,
Plumy tail, and wistful gaze
While you humoured our queer ways,
Or outshrilled your morning call
Up the stairs and through the hall—
Foot suspended in its fall—
While, expectant, you would stand
Arched, to meet the stroking hand;
Till your way you chose to wend
Yonder, to your tragic end.

Never another pet for me!
Let your place all vacant be;
Better blankness day by day
Than companion torn away.
Better bid his memory fade,
Better blot each mark he made,
Selfishly escape distress
By contrived forgetfulness,
Than preserve his prints to make
Every morn and eve an ache.

From the chair whereon he sat
Sweep his fur, nor wince thereat;
Rake his little pathways out
Mid the bushes roundabout;
Smooth away his talons' mark
From the claw-worn pine-tree bark,
Where he climbed as dusk embrowned,
Waiting us who loitered round.

Strange it is this speechless thing,
Subject to our mastering,
Subject for his life and food
To our gift, and time, and mood;
Timid pensioner of us Powers,
His existence ruled by ours,
Should—by crossing at a breath
Into safe and shielded death,
By the merely taking hence
Of his insignificance—
Loom as largened to the sense,
Shape as part, above man's will,
Of the Imperturbable.

As a prisoner, flight debarred,
Exercising in a yard,
Still retain I, troubled, shaken,
Mean estate, by him forsaken;
And this home, which scarcely took
Impress from his little look,
By his faring to the Dim
Grows all eloquent of him.

Housemate, I can think you still
Bounding to the window-sill,
Over which I vaguely see
Your small mound beneath the tree,
Showing in the autumn shade
That you moulder where you played.

—*Thomas Hardy*

The Erie Canal

I've got a mule, her name is Sal,
Fifteen years on the Erie Canal.
She's a good old worker and a good old pal,
Fifteen years on the Erie Canal.
We've hauled some barges in our day,
Filled with lumber, coal and hay.
And every inch of the way I know
From Albany to Buffalo.

Chorus
Low bridge, everybody down!
Low bridge, for we're comin' to a town!
You can always tell your neighbor, can always tell
*   your pal,*
If you've ever navigated on the Erie Canal.

We'd better look for a job, old gal,
Fifteen years on the Erie Canal.
You bet your life I wouldn't part with Sal,
Fifteen years on the Erie Canal.
Giddap there, Sal, we've passed that lock,
We'll make Rome 'fore six o'clock,
So one more trip and then we'll go
Right straight back to Buffalo.

Where would I be if I lost my pal?
Fifteen years on the Erie Canal.
Oh, I'd like to see a mule as good as Sal,
Fifteen years on the Erie Canal.
A friend of mine once got her sore,
Now he's got a broken jaw,
'Cause she let fly with her iron toe
And kicked him into Buffalo.

—*Anonymous*

The Cow

The friendly cow all red and white
   I love with all my heart:
She gives me cream with all her might,
   To eat with apple-tart.

She wanders lowing here and there,
   And yet she cannot stray,
All in the pleasant open air,
   The pleasant light of day;

And blown by all the winds that pass
   And wet with all the showers,
She walks among the meadow grass
   And eats the meadow flowers.

—*Robert Louis Stevenson*

Us Two

Wherever I am, there's always Pooh,
There's always Pooh and Me.
Whatever I do, he wants to do,
"Where are you going today?" says Pooh:
"Well, that's very odd 'cos I was too.
Let's go together," says Pooh, says he.
"Let's go together," says Pooh.

"What's twice eleven?" I said to Pooh.
("Twice what?" said Pooh to Me.)
"I *think* it ought to be twenty-two."
"Just what I think myself," said Pooh.
"It wasn't an easy sum to do,
But that's what it is," said Pooh, said he.
"That's what it is," said Pooh.

"Let's look for dragons," I said to Pooh.
"Yes, let's," said Pooh to Me.
We crossed the river and found a few—
"Yes, those are dragons all right," said Pooh.
"As soon as I saw their beaks I knew.

That's what they are," said Pooh, said he.
"That's what they are," said Pooh.

"Let's frighten the dragons," I said to Pooh.
"That's right," said Pooh to Me.
"*I'm* not afraid," I said to Pooh,
And I held his paw and I shouted "Shoo!
Silly old dragons!"—and off they flew.
"I wasn't afraid," said Pooh, said he,
"I'm *never* afraid with you."

So wherever I am, there's always Pooh,
There's always Pooh and Me.
"What would I do?" I said to Pooh,
"If it wasn't for you," and Pooh said: "True,
It isn't much fun for One, but Two
Can stick together," says Pooh, says he.
"That's how it is," says Pooh.

—*A. A. Milne*

FRIENDSHIP LOST

The Old Familiar Faces

I have had playmates, I have had companions,
In my days of childhood, in my joyful
   school-days;
All, all are gone, the old familiar faces.

I have been laughing, I have been carousing,
Drinking late, sitting late, with my bosom
   cronies;
All, all are gone, the old familiar faces.

I loved a Love once, fairest among women;
Closed are her doors on me, I must not see her—
All, all are gone, the old familiar faces.

I have a friend, a kinder friend has no man;
Like an ingrate, I left my friend abruptly;
Left him, to muse on the old familiar faces.

Ghost-like I paced round the haunts of my
    childhood.
Earth seem'd a desert I was bound to traverse,
Seeking to find the old familiar faces.

Friend of my bosom, thou more than a brother,
Why wert not thou born in my father's
    dwelling?
So might we talk of the old familiar faces—

How some they have died, and some they have
    left me,
And some are taken from me; all are departed;
All, all are gone, the old familiar faces.

—*Charles Lamb*

To a False Friend

Our hands have met, but not our hearts;
Our hands will never meet again.
Friends, if we have ever been,
Friends we cannot now remain:
I only know I loved you once,
I only know I loved in vain;
Our hands have met, but not our hearts;
Our hands will never meet again!

Then farewell to heart and hand!
I would our hands had never met:
Even the outward form of love
Must be resign'd with some regret.
Friends, we still might seem to be,
If I my wrong could e'er forget;
Our hands have join'd but not our hearts:
I would our hands had never met!

—*Thomas Hood*

Broken Friendship

Give me no gift! Less than thyself were nought.
It was thyself, alas! not thine I sought.
Once reigned I as a monarch in this heart,
Now from the doors a stranger I depart.

—*Mary Elizabeth Coleridge*

We Have Been Friends Together

We have been friends together
In sunshine and in shade,
Since first beneath the chestnut-tree,
In infancy we played.
But coldness dwells within thy heart;
A cloud is on thy brow;
We have been friends together—
Shall a light word part us now?

We have been gay together;
We have laughed at little jests;
For the fount of hope was gushing
Warm and joyous in our breasts,
But laughter now hath fled thy lip,
And sullen glooms thy brow;
We have been gay together—
Shall a light word part us now?

We have been sad together;
We have wept with bitter tears
O'er the grass-grown graves where slumbered
The hopes of early years.
The voices which are silent there
Would bid thee clear thy brow;
We have been sad together—
Oh! what shall part us now?

—*Caroline Elizabeth Sarah Norton*

A Lost Friend

My friend he was; my friend from all the rest;
With childish faith he oped to me his breast.
No door was locked on altar, grave or grief;
No weakness veiled, concealed, no disbelief;
The hope, the sorrow, and the wrong were
   bare,
And, ah, the shadow only showed the fair.

I gave him love for love, but deep within,
I magnified each frailty into sin;
Each hill-topped foible in the sunset glowed,
Obscuring vales where rivered virtues flowed.
Reproof became reproach, till common grew
The captious word at every fault I knew.
He smiled upon the censorship, and bore
With patient love the touch that wounded sore;
Until at length, so had my blindness grown,
He knew I judged him by his faults alone.

Alone of all men, I who knew him best,
Refused the gold, to take the dross for test!
Cold strangers honored for the worth they saw;

His friend forgot the diamond in the flaw.
At last it came—the day he stood apart,
When from my eyes he proudly veiled his
    heart;
When carping judgment and uncertain word
A stern resentment in his bosom stirred;
When in his face I read what I had been
And with his vision I saw what he had seen.

Too late! Too late! Oh, could he then have
    known,
When his love died, that mine had perfect
    grown;
That when the veil was drawn, abased,
    chastised,
The censor stood, and the lost one truly prized.

Too late we learn—a man must hold his friend
Unjudged, accepted, trusted to the end.

—*John Boyle O'Reilly*

The Fire of Driftwood

Devereux Farm, near Marblehead

We sat within the farm-house old,
   Whose windows, looking o'er the bay,
Gave to the sea-breeze damp and cold,
   An easy entrance, night and day.

Not far away we saw the port,
   The strange, old-fashioned, silent town,
The lighthouse, the dismantled fort,
   The wooden houses, quaint and brown.

We sat and talked until the night,
   Descending, filled the little room;
Our faces faded from the sight,
   Our voices only broke the gloom.

We spake of many a vanished scene,
   Of what we once had thought and said,
Of what had been, and might have been,
   And who was changed, and who was dead;

And all that fills the hearts of friends,
  When first they feel, with secret pain,
Their lives thenceforth have separate ends,
  And never can be one again;

The first slight swerving of the heart,
  That words are powerless to express,
And leave it still unsaid in part,
  Or say it in too great excess.

The very tones in which we spake
  Had something strange, I could but mark;
The leaves of memory seemed to make
  A mournful rustling in the dark.

Oft died the words upon our lips,
  As suddenly, from out the fire
Built of the wreck of stranded ships,
  The flames would leap and then expire.

And, as their splendor flashed and failed,
    We thought of wrecks upon the main,
Of ships dismasted, that were hailed
    And sent no answer back again.

The windows, rattling in their frames,
    The ocean, roaring up the beach,
The gusty blast, the bickering flames,
    All mingled vaguely in our speech;

Until they made themselves a part
    Of fancies floating through the brain,
The long-lost ventures of the heart,
    That send no answers back again.

O flames that glowed! O hearts that yearned!
    They were indeed too much akin,
The drift-wood fire without that burned,
    The thoughts that burned and glowed within.

—*Henry Wadsworth Longfellow*

Poem

I loved my friend.
He went away from me.
There's nothing more to say.
The poem ends,
Soft as it began,
I loved my friend.

—*Langston Hughes*

When We Two Parted

When we two parted
  In silence and tears,
Half broken-hearted
  To sever for years,
Pale grew thy cheek and cold,
  Colder thy kiss;
Truly that hour foretold
  Sorrow to this.

The dew of the morning
  Sunk chill on my brow—
It felt like the warning
  Of what I feel now.
Thy vows are all broken,
  And light is thy fame;
I hear thy name spoken,
  And share in its shame.

They name thee before me,
   A knell to mine ear;
A shudder comes o'er me—
   Why wert thou so dear?
They know not I knew thee,
   Who knew thee too well—
Long, long shall I rue thee,
   Too deeply to tell.

In secret we met—
   In silence I grieve
That thy heart could forget,
   Thy spirit deceive.
If I should meet thee
   After long years,
How should I greet thee?—
   With silence and tears.

—*George Gordon, Lord Byron*

Nobody Knows You When You're Down and Out

Once I lived the life of a millionaire
Spent all my money, I just didn't care
Taking my friends out for a mighty fine time
Drinking high-priced liquor, champagne and
  wine.
When I began to fall so low
I didn't have a friend and no place to go
If I ever get my hands on a dollar again
I'm gonna hang on to it till that eagle grins

Nobody knows you
When you're down and out.
In your pocket, not one penny,
And your friends, you haven't any.
But as soon as you finally get on your feet again
Ev'rybody wants to be your long lost friend
It's mighty strange, without a doubt,
Nobody knows you when you're down and out.

—*Jimmie Cox*

Money

When I had money, money, O!
  I knew no joy till I went poor;
For many a false man as a friend
  Came knocking all day at my door.

Then felt I like a child that holds
  A trumpet that he must not blow
Because a man is dead; I dared
  Not speak to let this false world know.

Much have I thought of life, and seen
  How poor men's hearts are ever light;
And how their wives do hum like bees
  About their work from morn till night.

So, when I hear these poor ones laugh,
  And see the rich ones coldly frown—
Poor men, think I, need not go up
  So much as rich men should come down.

When I had money, money, O!
    My many friends proved all untrue;
But now I have no money, O!
    My friends are real though very few.

—*W. H. Davies*

Since Hanna Moved Away

The tires on my bike are flat.
The sky is grouchy gray.
At least it sure feels like that
Since Hanna moved away.

Chocolate ice cream tastes like prunes.
December's come to stay.
They've taken back the Mays and Junes
Since Hanna moved away.

Flowers smell like halibut.
Velvet feels like hay.
Every handsome dog's a mutt
Since Hanna moved away.

Nothing's fun to laugh about.
Nothing's fun to play.
They call me, but I won't come out
Since Hanna moved away.

—*Judith Viorst*

Taking Leave of a Friend

Blue mountains lie beyond the north wall;
Round the city's eastern side flows the white
    water.
Here we part, friend, once forever.
You go ten thousand miles, drifting away
Like an unrooted water-grass.
Oh, the floating clouds and the thoughts of a
    wanderer!
Oh, the sunset and the longing of an old friend!
We ride away from each other, waving our hands,
While our horses neigh softly, softly . . .

—*Li Po*
Translated from the Chinese by Shigeyoshi Obata

Heart's House

My heart is but a little house
With room for only three or four,
And it was filled before you knocked
Upon the door.

I longed to bid you come within,
I knew that I should love you well,
But if you came the rest must go
Elsewhere to dwell.

And so, farewell, O friend, my friend!
Nay, I could weep a little too,
But I shall only smile and say
Farewell to you.

—*Sara Teasdale*

IN MEMORIAM

I Go, Sweet Friends

I go, sweet friends! yet think of me
When spring's young voice awakes with flowers;
For we have wandered far and free
In those bright hours, the violet's hours.

I go; but when you pause to hear
From distant hills the Sabbath-bell
On summer-winds float silvery clear,
Think on me then—I loved it well!

Forget me not around your hearth,
When cheerly smiles the ruddy blaze;
For dear hath been its evening mirth
To me, sweet friends, in other days.

And oh! when music's voice is heard
To melt in strains of parting woe,
When hearts to love and grief are stirred,
Think of me then! I go, I go!

—*Felicia Dorothea Hemans*

Remember

Remember me when I am gone away,
   Gone far away into the silent land;
   When you can no more hold me by the hand,
Nor I half turn to go yet turning stay.
Remember me when no more day by day
   You tell me of our future that you planned:
   Only remember me; you understand
It will be late to counsel then or pray.
Yet if you should forget me for a while
   And afterwards remember, do not grieve:
   For if the darkness and corruption leave
   A vestige of the thoughts that once I had,
Better by far you should forget and smile
   Than that you should remember and be sad.

—*Christina Georgina Rossetti*

If Anybody's Friend Be Dead

If anybody's friend be dead
It's sharpest of the theme
The thinking how they walked alive—
At such and such a time—

Their costume, of a Sunday,
Some manner of the Hair—
A prank nobody knew but them,
Lost, in the Sepulchre.

How warm, they were, on such a day,
You almost feel the date—
So short way off it seems—
And now—they're Centuries from that—

How pleased they were, at what you said—
You try to touch the smile
And dip your fingers in the frost—
When was it—Can you tell—

You asked the Company to tea—
Acquaintance—just a few—
And chatted close with this Grand Thing
That don't remember you—

Past Bows, and Invitations—
Past Interview, and Vow—
Past what Ourself can estimate—
That—makes the Quick of Woe!

—*Emily Dickinson*

A Legacy

Friend of my many years!
When the great silence falls, at last, on me,
Let me not leave, to pain and sadden thee,
A memory of tears,

But pleasant thoughts alone
Of one who was thy friendship's honored guest
And drank the wine of consolation pressed
From sorrows of thy own.

I leave with thee a sense
Of hands upheld and trials rendered less—
The unselfish joy which is to helpfulness
Its own great recompense;

The knowledge that from thine,
As from the garments of the Master, stole
Calmness and strength, the virtue which makes
  whole
And heals without a sign;

Yea more, the assurance strong
That love, which fails of perfect utterance here,
Lives on to fill the heavenly atmosphere
With its immortal song.

—*John Greenleaf Whittier*

My Legacy

My friend has gone away from me
From shadow into perfect light,
But leaving a sweet legacy.

My heart shall hold it long in fee
A grand ideal, calm and bright,
A song of hope for ministry,

A faith of unstained purity,
A thought of beauty for delight
These did my friend bequeath to me;

And, more than even these can be,
The worthy pattern of a white,
Unmarred life lived most graciously.

Dear comrade, loyal thanks to thee
Who now hath fared beyond my sight,
My friend has gone away from me,
But leaving a sweet legacy.

—*Lucy Maud Montgomery*

On Parting with a Friend

Can I forget thee? No, while mem'ry lasts,
Thine image like a talisman entwined,
Around my heart by sacred friendship's ties
Remains unchanged, in love, pure love, enshrined.

Can I forget thee? Childhood's happy hours
Would like some flitting phantom mock and jeer;
Life's sunny hours, would quickly lose their
   charm,
If Lethe's slumbrous waves but touched me there.

Can I forget thee? 'Tis a sad, sad thought,
That friend from friend should thus be ruthless
   riven—
But list, methinks, a sweet voice whispers low,
Remember, no adieus are spoke in heaven.

Can I forget thee? No, though ocean's waves
May madly leap and foam 'twixt you and me,
Still o'er my stricken heart this yearning will
   remain,
Nor time estrange my love, dear one, from thee.

And though on earth again we never more may
   meet,
In that bright Elysian where spirits, holy, dwell,
May we in concert with that transported throng,
Unite, ne'er more (rapt thought) to say
   "farewell!"

—*Mary Weston Fordham*

Epitaph on a Friend

Oh Friend! for ever loved, for ever dear!
What fruitless tears have bathed thy honour'd
    bier!
What sighs re-echo'd to thy parting breath,
Whilst thou wast struggling in the pangs of
    death!
Could tears retard the tyrant in his course;
Could sighs avert his dart's relentless force;
Could youth and virtue claim a short delay,
Or beauty charm the spectre from his prey;
Thou still hadst lived to bless my aching sight,
Thy comrades honour and thy friend's delight.
If yet thy gentle spirit hover nigh
The spot where now thy moldering ashes lie,
Here wilt thou read, recorded on my heart,
A grief too deep to trust the sculptor's art.
No marble marks thy couch of lowly sleep,
But living statues there are seen to weep;

Affliction's semblance bends not o'er thy tomb,
Affliction's self deplores thy youthful doom.
What though thy sire lament his failing line,
A father's sorrows cannot equal mine!
Though none, like thee, his dying hour will cheer,
Yet other offspring soothe his anguish here:
But, who with me shall hold thy former place?
Thine image, what new friendship can efface?
Ah! non!—a father's tears will cease to flow,
Time will assuage an infant brother's woe;
To all, save one, is consolation known,
While solitary friendship sighs alone.

—*George Gordon, Lord Byron*

Lines To Mrs. Isabel Peace

'Tis said but a name is friendship,
Soulless, and shallow, and vain;
That the human heart ne'er beats in response,
Or echoes sweet sympathy's strain.

But to-day in "memory's mirror"
Came a dear and honored one,
Whom in days gone by had lived and had loved,
Ere her heavenly goal was won.

Her countenance beamed as of yore,
With radiant smiles of love,
And I felt that the friendship she lavished me
    here,
Had ripened in heaven above.

I felt that her voice so winsome,
Attuned to holier rhymes,
Would in soft cadence tell of friendship's truth,
Like harp of a thousand strings.

Rise up and call her blest!
Ye children of her love,
For a friendlier hand or a kindlier heart
Ne'er entered the mansions above.

—*Mary Weston Fordham*

The Word

My friend, my bonny friend, when we are old,
    And hand in hand go tottering down the hill,
May we be rich in love's refined gold,
    May love's gold coin be current with us still.

May love be sweeter for the vanished days,
    And your most perfect beauty still as dear
As when your troubled singer stood at gaze
    In the dear March of a most sacred year.

May what we are be all we might have been,
    And that potential, perfect, Oh my friend,
And may there still be many sheafs to glean
    In our love's acre, comrade, till the end.

And may we find, when ended is the page
Death but a tavern on our pilgrimage.

—*John Masefield*

Of his Dear Son, Gervase

Dear Lord, receive my son, whose winning love
To me was like a friendship, far above
The course of nature or his tender age;
Whose looks could all my bitter griefs assuage:
Let his pure soul, ordain'd seven years to be
In that frail body which was part of me,
Remain my pledge in Heaven, as sent to show
How to this port at every step I go.

—*Sir John Beaumont*

Around the Corner

Around the corner I have a friend,
In this great city that has no end;
Yet days go by, and weeks rush on,
And before I know it, a year is gone,
And I never see my old friend's face,
For Life is a swift and terrible race.
He knows I like him just as well
As in the days when I rang his bell
And he rang mine.
We were younger then,
And now we are busy, tired men:
Tired with playing a foolish game,
Tired with trying to make a name.
"To-morrow," I say, "I will call on Jim,
Just to show that I'm thinking of him."
But to-morrow comes—and to-morrow goes,
And the distance between us grows and grows.

Around the corner!—yet miles away . . .
"Here's a telegram, sir,"
   "Jim died to-day."

And that's what we get, and deserve in the end:
Around the corner, a vanished friend.

—*Charles Hanson Towne*

An Old Story

Strange that I did not know him then,
   That friend of mine!
I did not even show him then
   One friendly sign;

But cursed him for the ways he had
   To make me see
My envy of the praise he had
   For praising me.

I would have rid the earth of him
   Once, in my pride . . .
I never knew the worth of him
   Until he died.

—*Edwin Arlington Robinson*

The Friend Who Just "Stands By"

When trouble comes your soul to try,
You love the friend who just "stands by."
Perhaps there's nothing he can do—
The thing is strictly up to you;
For there are troubles all your own,
And paths the soul must tread alone;
Times when love cannot smooth the road
Nor friendship lift the heavy load,
But just to know you have a friend
Who will "stand by" until the end,
Whose sympathy through all endures,
Whose warm handclasp is always yours—
It helps, someway, to pull you through,
Although there's nothing he can do.
And so with fervent heart you cry,
"God bless the friend who just 'stands by'!"

—*B. Y. Williams*

PERMISSIONS
ACKNOWLEDGMENTS ~~~~

INDEX OF AUTHORS

Adams, St. Clair, 60
Alfred, Lord Tennyson, 30
Anonymous, 36–37, 54, 61, 158–159, 163–164
Auden, W. H., 81–83
Author unknown, 49–50

Belloc, Hilaire, 22
Beaumont, Sir John, 206
Black, Baxter, 56–57
Brizieux, Julien Auguste Pelage, 156
Brontë, Emily, 136
Brooks, Maria A., 33–34
Browning, Elizabeth Barrett, 146–154
Browning, Robert, 140–141
Burns, Robert, 86, 131

Campbell, Anne, 74
Carlyle, Thomas, 28
Carver, Raymond, 70–71
Cary, Alice, 101–105
Cheke, Henry, 6
Coatsworth, Elizabeth, 145
Coleridge, Hartley, 118, 124
Coleridge, Mary Elizabeth, 173
Cox, Jimmie, 184
Craik, Dinah Maria Mulock, iv

Davidson, Lucretia Maria, 21
Davies, Mary Carolyn, 121
Davies, W. H., 185–186
Dawson, Grace Stricker, 108–109

de Vere, Aubrey Thomas, 87
de Vere, Mary Ainge, 132
Dickinson, Emily, 194–195
Dobson, Henry Austin, 114
Dunbar, Paul Laurence, 51

Emerson, Ralph Waldo, 120

Fordham, Mary Weston, 199–200, 203–204
Free, Spencer Michael, 20
Frost, Robert, 55

Gibran, Kahlil, 26–27
Gilder, Richard Watson, 46
Gordon, George, Lord Byron, 182–183, 201–202
Grafly, Dorothy, 111–112
Grimald, Nicholas, 2–4
Guiterman, Arthur, 155

Hardy, Thomas, 93, 160–162
Hartzell, Ruth A., 17
Hemans, Felicia Dorothea, 14–15, 192
Holmes, Oliver Wendell, 94–97
Hood, Thomas, 172
Howard, Henry, Earl of Surrey, 117
Howe, Julia Ward, 79–80
Hughes, Langston, 181

Johnson, Samuel, 13
Jonson, Ben, 75–77

Kahn, Gus, 58–59
Kassia, 48
Kipling, Rudyard, 31–32

Lamb, Charles, 170–171
Larcom, Lucy, 10–12
Longfellow, Henry Wadsworth, 66–67, 106, 178–180
Lowell, Amy, 119

Masefield, John, 135, 205
Millay, Edna St. Vincent, 137
Milne, A. A., 72, 167
Montgomery, Lucy Maud, 198

Nesbit, Wilbur D., 7–9
Norton, Caroline Elizabeth Sarah, 174–175

O'Reilly, John Boyle, 176–177

Parry, Joseph, 29
Peacock, Molly, 62–63
Po, Chü-I, 91–92
Po, Li, 188
Porter, Cole, 52–53

Quarles, Francis, 44–45

Riley, James Whitcomb, 115–116
Robinson, Edwin Arlington, 209

Rossetti, Christina Georgina, 133–134, 193
Rowe, Nicholas, 5

Shakespeare, William, 88, 113
Shelley, Percy Bysshe, 16
Shoshone Love Song, 138
Smith, Stevie, 23
Stevenson, Robert Louis, 125, 165
Sui, Ch'eng-Kung, 78

Teasdale, Sara, 35, 189
Thoreau, Henry David, 38–41
Towne, Charles Hanson, 207–208

Ŭm-gil, Ŏm, 73

van Dyke, Henry, 68–69
Viorst, Judith, 187

Ward, B. J., 89–90
Watson, William, 157
Whitman, Walt, 42–43
Whittier, John Greenleaf, 197
Wilcox, Ella Wheeler, 98–100, 122–123, 128–130, 139
Williams, B. Y., 210
Wyatt, Sir Thomas, 144

Yeats, William Butler, 18–19, 110

INDEX OF FIRST LINES

A little health, 54
A quiet valley with no man's footprints, 73
After so long an absence, 66
After the fierce midsummer all ablaze, 139
All's over, then: does truth sound bitter, 140
And a youth said, Speak to us of Friendship, 26
Around the corner I have a friend, 207
As when with downcast eyes we muse and brood, 30
At night I dreamt I was back in Ch'ang-an; 91

Being her friend, I do not care, not I, 135
Blue mountains lie beyond the north wall; 188
But rifling through the old one, 89

Can I forget thee? No, while mem'ry lasts, 199
Come, dear old comrade, you and I, 94

Dear Lord, receive my son, whose winning love to me was like a friendship, 206

Fair is the white star of twilight, 138

Friend is a word that I don't throw around, 56
Friend of my many years!, 196
Friend of my youth, let us talk of old times; 98
Friendship needs no studied phrases, 36
Friendship. Peculiar boon of heav'n, 13
Friendship's like music; two strings tuned alike, 44

Give me no gift! Less than thyself were nought, 173

He sits and begs, he gives a paw, 155
His friends he loved. His direst earthly foes—, 157

I ask but one thing of you, only one, 119
I go, sweet friends! Yet think of me, 192
I have had playmates, I have had companions, 170
I knew it the first of the Summer—, 128
I love life in all its phases, 17
I loved my friend, 181
I read, dear friend, in your dear face, 125
I saw in Louisiana a live-oak growing, 42

I sent out invitations, 78
I shot an arrow into the air, 106
I think awhile of Love, and while
    I think, 38
I went by footpath and by stile, 93
If anybody's friend be dead, 194
If I had known what trouble you
    were bearing; 121
If you're ever in a jam, here I am,
    52
Is it you, Jack? Old boy, is it
    really you?, 101
It is a sweet thing, friendship, a
    dear balm, 16
I've got a mule, her name is Sal,
    163

Jim and I as children played
    together, 61

Life is a book that we study, 58
Life is but a troubled ocean, 21
Love is like the wild rose-briar;
    136
Loving friend, the gift of one, 146
Lux, my fair falcon, and your fel-
    lows all, 144

Make new friemds, but keep the
    old; 29
My friend has gone away from
    me, 198
My friend he was; my friend from
    all the rest; 176
My friend, my bonny friend,
    when we are old, 205
My friend, the things that do
    attain, 117

My heart is but a little house,
    189

Now must I these three praise—,
    18

O friend, my bosom said, 120
O friend, we sit together, and the
    room, 111
O who will walk a mile with me,
    68
Of all the heavenly gifts that
    mortal men commend, 2
Oh Friend! For ever loved, for
    ever dear!, 201
Oh! Friendship, sweetest, exqui-
    site delight, 14
Oh, the comfort—the inexpress-
    ible comfort of feeling safe
    with a person, iv
Old friends are best! And so to
    you, 114
Once fondly lov'd, and still
    remember'd dear, 131
Once I lived the life of a million-
    aire, 184
One man in a thousand, Solomon
    says, 31
Our hands have met, but not our
    hearts; 172
Ours yet not ours, being set
    apart, 81

Pangar, my white cat, and I,
    158
Pet was never mourned as you,
    160
Promise me no promises, 133

Remember me when I am gone
    away, 193

Should auld acquaintance be for-
    got, 86
So early it's still almost dark out,
    70
Strange that I did not know him
    then, 209

The eve I came the dog 'gan bark;
    156
The friendly cow all red and
    white, 165
The half-seen memories of child-
    ish days, 87
The pleasures of friendship are
    exquisite, 23
The tires on my bike are flat.,
    187
There is always a place for you at
    my table, 74
There's all of pleasure and all of
    peace, 7
They came to tell your faults to
    me, 35
They say that in the unchanging
    place, 22
They tell me I am shrewd with
    other men; 79
Though you are in your shining
    days, 110
Thrice is sweet music sweet
    when every word, 46
Throwing out old clothes is
    painful, 62
'Tis better to sit here beside the
    sea, 51

'Tis said but a name is friendship,
    203
'Tis the human touch in this
    world that counts, 20
To me, fair friend, you never can
    be old, 113
To meet a friendship such as
    mine, 33
Tonight, grave sir, both my poor
    house, and I, 75
True friends, 28
True friendship unfeign?d, 6

We have been friends together,
    174
We parted on the mountains, as
    two streams, 124
We sat within the farm-house
    old, 178
We talk of taxes, and I call you
    friend; 137
We were just three, 145
What is the best a friend can be,
    10
When a feller hasn't got a cent, 49
When a friend calls to me from
    the road, 55
When Anne and I go out a walk,
    72
When I had money, money, O!,
    185
When Psyche's friend becomes
    her lover, 132
When to the sessions of sweet
    silent thought, 88
When trouble comes your soul to
    try, 210
When we two parted, 182

When we were idlers with the loitering rills, 118

Wherever I am, there's always Pooh, 166

Who knows the joys of friendship?, 5

You entered my life in a casual way, 108

You meet your friend, your face, 48

"You're a friend of mine, or I wouldn't ask," 60

You've a manner all so mellow, 115

Your words came just when needed., 122